MW01602315

I forgot to tell you

❧

I forgot to tell you

❦

gillian harding-russell

thistledown press

©gillian harding-russell, 2007
All rights reserved

No part of this publication may be reproduced or transmitted in any form or by any means,
graphic, electronic or mechanical, including photocopying, recording, or any information
storage and retrieval system, without permission in writing from the publisher or a licence
from The Canadian Copyright Licensing Agency (Accesss Copyright). For an Access
Copyright licence, visit www.accesscopyright.ca or call toll free to 1-800-893-5777.

Library and Archives Canada Cataloguing in Publication

Harding-Russell, Gillian, 1952-
I forgot to tell you / Gillian Harding-Russell.

Poems.
ISBN 978-1-897235-34-8

I. Title.

PS8565.A632312 2007   C811'.54   C2007-904538-3

Cover photograph ©Gregor Schuster/zefa/Corbis
Cover and book design by Jackie Forrie
Printed and bound in Canada

Thistledown Press Ltd.
633 Main Street
Saskatoon, Saskatchewan, S7H 0J8
www.thistledownpress.com

 Canada Council   Conseil des Arts Canadian   Patrimoine
for the Arts   du Canada   Heritage   canadien

Thistledown Press gratefully acknowledges the financial assistance of the Canada Council
for the Arts, the Saskatchewan Arts Board, and the Government of Canada through the
Book Publishing Industry Development Program for its publishing program.

ACKNOWLEDGEMENTS

I would like to thank the Saskatchewan Writers' Guild for awarding "Nothing Prepared me for Winter" first prize in the poetry section of the 2005 literary Competition, and "Roses, Lovers and God" (renamed "Rose in March") first place in the 2006 competition. "Among the poplar, sometimes birds" won second prize in the "summer theme" *New Quarterly* contest (2004). I am obliged to the editors of Three Square Press for publishing excerpts from the "Dragon poems" series in the anthology *The Common Sky: Poems against the US-led Invasion of Iraq* (2003). I would like to thank *Grain* for publishing "Corner of Fleet and Victoria," and *Event Magazine* for featuring "Heart, and "Nothing Prepared me for Winter" in an honorary Fall, 2005 issue. Again, thanks to *Transition* magazine for publishing "Thought, Unbidden" in their Fall 2006 issue, and thanks to Cranberry Press for including "II . . . from an ambush" from the longer poem "The undercover war drags on" in the anthology *Reportage*. Also thanks to the *Dalhousie Review* for including "Resourses for Pain" in their summer 2007 issue. I would like to thank Susan Musgrave for her receptive but astute eye, and David Zieroth for his ongoing advice and encouragement.

CONTENTS

From "Report"

. . .

A self-delusion when building sandcastles, collecting postage stamps, admiring oneself in a mirror.

Assigning oneself first place in sport, power, love, and the getting of money.

All the while on the very border, on the fragile border beyond which there is a province of mumblings and wails.

For in every one of us a mad rabbit thrashes and a wolf pack howls, so that we are afraid it will be heard by others.

— Czeslaw Milosz
New and Collected Poems

From "Standard Oil Co."

However entangled the petroleum's
arteries may be, however the layers
may change their silent site
and move their sovereignty
amid the earth's bowels,
when the fountain gushes
its paraffin foliage,
Standard Oil arrived beforehand
with its checks and its guns,
and its governments and its prisoners.

— Pablo Neruda
The Poetry of Pablo Neruda

Star conductor
(*for Peter*)

Snow's glittering shawl wrapped round the curve
of the driveway where the old car juts
shining white in starlight this two-faced January
thaw and blizzard together
tomorrow we will be
apart

Now your palm's hot shadow
on the small of my back,
sacrum seat of the soul
triangular, remote
controlled
sends sparks   flying
up the column of the spine

Venus high
in the western sky   diamond fire
by my right temple, Mars' flare
lower to the south, sinistral
fears infiltrating the left ear.

You point out Orion's fading jewelled shoulder,
Betelgeuse and Rigel still bright
at the starry belt more than 1000 light years
beyond ourselves standing small on Earth

(Sirius, brightest dog star,
protector of Virgo, waits out the seasons
while you conduct this silent orchestra
rearranging constellations   columbine
gatherings in synaptic   star trees
and I, perennially blind,
trace

in my mind
just these fragile nerve strings, pearls   unstrung —)

Distances

Stitch by stitch the frost
travels across the windshield,

the ignition won't turn
over, the windshield wipers

aslant in mid-orbit, mid-thought
waiting for you to arrive with

the red-wired booster cable
to loop a circuit of embrace

outside Warehouse One where
across the street the air is   visible

a pillar of salt   frozen smoke
grey in front of our faces, looked back at

as we whitely breathe out — smoking, stinking tail pipes
fiery dragons or not-so-fictive dinosaurs

that once walked the earth, all this metal and exhaust
left behind us.

ii

Molecules interlock
dendrites of frost creeping fingers of ice

stitch by stitch, forming across the lake to the deepest blue
of danger

where we skated over ice last Sunday
flash of blade and sunlight

on your face
laughing out loud

(beneath our feet   fishes
slow flicker thoughts, gills   wave gently

weeds frozen movement nosing under a sheet of ice
into sand head-rifts postponing thought until
spring   thaw   dislodges).

iii

And roughly 354 kilometres above our heads
through ocean leagues of sky   the International Space Station
three astronauts are marooned pending a rescue shuttle
after the Challenger exploded 30 kilometres above Florida
coming down through azure walls of sky,
remnants to the border of Texas.

Someone reported to have pointed out
the glimmering blue-green ball, entranced
by its swirling beauty bathed in marble clouds
soon after take off
(A journey ago

the moment before
re-entering . . .) blue, blue   atmosphere
sheet of quality vellum
of equatorial sky, anticipating the first
unsteady foot on the ground.
Explosion that takes
the place of thought
and the world
to precede it?

iv

Back on shivering Earth, I watch you
beside me, hooking up batteries, bent over

the car hood generating all that is   sublimation
and gaseous   evaporation   desire
unravelling fetal wisps
secret codes coagulating   random drops
of condensation

molecules still interlocking hands
and love still holding the solid world
together

Risking the avalanche

I   Snow

is the sky
condensed / translated
rendered solid
for human consumption.

(reached for
round the jaw of a ledge
between incisors of rock
spiralling upwards).

II   Immanence

From the razor edge of horizon
towards the inland reaches of the will

to cross (outdistance)   oneself
towards the wide, open spaces
of faith, a snowy altar
come

face to face
with the saw-toothed edge
of danger

experience the long pull
slide   forward
gluteus medius and *gluteus maximus, abductor*
magnus, vastus lateralis
(self inside, lock

of joints, the easy
muscles flowing through
the facile   spreading   body)
with the little flights
down
between slopes

the weightlessness of bones . . .

Always looking back up
at the man in the moon look-alike: glaciered mountain top
between granite precipices

rift of snow
infinite hilarity in the long-snouted smile
(sliced by the darker shadow of a sneer?)

the roar and a full-throated laughter across
the ancient cradle of a canyon
ten seconds human warning
just to catch

                           a glimpse

 . . . and already it's too late.

Phobos Portfolio

!

Anxiety in the green sign post
that points the wrong way

(you will have deciphered
 the letters, cryptic backwards

as well as straight forwards, read
the white place names luminescent under

shadow of dusk, turning
dark, concluded irrefutably

you are going in a direction you had not
planned, but there is no going
back you are going, going

forward, propelled
by Something outside / inside

yourself . . .)
on the way there —

!!

Fear in a shining, black
raincoat, memory

of raindrops leaden
drop, dropping on the windshield

the day the shock-white van crashed
a lightning bolt through the side

door of your car, crushed in
like a broken wing, turning

left out of the side road
your flicker

left on. And there is dread
in the bare empty spaces of abrasive grey road
ever after

reluctance to drive on certain clammier days
or at night when there is fear

in the accidental stick
kicked

by your right foot
on a wayward night pavement

fraying curl of exhaust
a snake of infernal wisdom, beckoning
or warning

under the hood of the brain
stem, gravel of a conjecture

where the noise   the squeal of . . .
 . . . tires is always

(remembered) before
it is heard . . .

                !!!

Fear in the fenced-in
hayfield, the horse sent off
to pasture

empty yellow stalks dry
as old hair, and fear in

the cow's placid cud, teeth
slimed green with grass out

in the middle of nowhere when you don't
know the way, and the sun

is a feverish ghost gauzed over
in summer cloud. And the hot air is heavy, heavy
                                    with molecules

held in a million infinitesimal hands
that hold you static

without direction or
desire to break away

escape you inwardly
distrust . . .

                    !v

Fear in a cow when fellow
carcasses may be chopped up

into its vegetable feed
to make it bigger and better and beefier

and Man creates the source
of his own fear, custom —

makes disease out
of the un-

natural. If there was once a lingering fear
and disgust in a slab of steak that conjures up

once muscled flesh, forget
the living animal (solemn chewing

its cud) ruminating waves over a yellow-stubble field
in the heat of summer above

your own labouring jaw
and all the steps and processes

between — what can there be now
but anxiety for such a victim

when the field of carcasses
bears the odour of your own sins?

v

Anxiety in an eyeball's
microcosmic world moving in, moving in
too close, too close . . .

. . . *Big Bang gathering momentum*
moving out, moving out . . .

centrifugal /centripetal
world (not seen the way it
used to be . . .) zooming in and out
of
focus

through the long dark of a pupil infiltrating the deep-sea cable
of a swollen optic nerve through channels of jellyfish brain

when you will have read too long
letters of pain, too wet, too dark,
inflamed on receiving acres of retina, sucked under
the swell of too many worlds

. . . the whirr of too many words.

but there is prayer in the naked eyeball
behind its veil of misty molecule, wraiths
of past considerations   sifting   through sight
spark of
angel

black   speck
aureole of light   shooting through

> the inward-seeing, underwater eye
> all light and airy

> where fish once ruled the world.

v!

Fear in the full moon
sullied and suffused with the hue
of blood in May

superimposed by the devil's dark hump
(black as sackcloth over the sun
eclipsed)

has the power to call off
armies, bring about a truce
after five war-torn years

that could be a sign
of something (everything means
something and nobody knows) the invisible
workings of the universe
registered in the inward-crawling

outward guts of our destinies.
Fear doubt/hope
makes us think

twice, transpose one thought
over another thought

change our minds
once again.

v!!

Mercury passing over the sun's massive eye
a far distant fleck

less frequent than heart attack or stroke (passing twelve times
a century)

like an ant crawling over the roof of the Agridome
reminding us of the incredible   distance
between

Earth and the life-giving sun, humming
in spitfire frequency, circuit-paralysing flares
every eleven years. Mercury, dark pupil of the sun, speeding up
                                        to dilate   space / time

warped, expanding like a bright idea, adjusting within the tilting
time-frame of its own nimble axis
and frame of reference.

Magnatar with a magnetic field of 1000 trillion gauss
competing tectonic plates wrestling
in star-quake, explodes   Supernova
implodes . . .

come as Revelation
on the Day of the Dinosaur.

On the Day of Man.

                v!!!

Anxiety in the basement
of stored memory, all the clutter

climbing up the dog-haired stairs
emptying into the garage of broken

parts, stench of oil and gasoline pouring
onto the suburban street, all the surfaces

of the present house covered with plaque
between the lost teeth of intention, nooks

and cavities filled with the grout of past
lives or selves that have not taken

root (decay in the interstices of pink gums
between the incisors of resolution — gingivitis, tartar

pyorrhea — ultimately thrombotic). Toys
from a decade ago: tricolour rattle, the magnetic

alphabet letters stuck to the refrigerator re-
discovered in a rusted soup can, one-legged Barbie

backwards bending at the waist, teddy
ear-torn and one-eyed, sideways

swimming lugubrious on the dusty shelf
above the discarded TV and garage-sale computer

moved to this dim-lit world of subatomic
memory. And your own clay hands to lift up

the detritus of the past become leaden
under an infernal weight of dust.

       !x

Fear as small as a deer mouse
trapped behind the stove

having dragged kibbles of dry dog food,
tasty crumb of cookie or macaroni shell

across the measured squares of kitchen linoleum, stacked high
behind the plastic bowl of a colander letting in

trellised four o'clock light
beside a lost silver dessert spoon,

smudged and murky concave mirror
for a miniature Uruk-hai warrior

inside this secret refuge. Fear a musty smell
from somewhere down the drain

pipe snake unable to reach
under the sink you knew you

suspected you looked for
it three times couldn't find

the cause. Fear the reek and rat
ferment and fear of contagion: Hantavirus,

the plague and
final soul rot.

x

Anxiety in the sudden collar of fire
round your throat, hot blasts
of SARS, Ebola, West Nile, Avian Flu or some other
unnamed, evolving monstrous under the microscope
three heads and nine eyes of ill will.
Shrill scratch of an icicle nail
flu: bewitched
circle of infection
passed on by the touch
of love, kiss or caress . . . *Ring around*

the Rosies /pocket full of posies . . .
Doctor wearing beaked headdress filled with daisies
or flimsy latex-trimmed mask
with elastic band to ward off
Contagion hurled down . . . with stardust, life-giving
or destroying . . .

so that in finding yourself sick and driving
feverish on a barren road you are alone
aware of the dimness of the car ahead, white
afternoon light   opaque

without lustre, knowing
floods will follow droughts
coughs, colds coming
with fevers and that

the mirage at the dip in the highway
so unmistakable, a warning
there may be dangers, tricks
blind spots, ambushes of deceived hope
you are bound to die of
or its opposite

regardless
below the rawness of a throat looked down into — inviting entry
past the epiglottis, dangling
inert

heart-shaped cavern
to swallow you up.

x!

Stand aside while we demolish the place . . .

(Did they telephone first, let it
ring and get no answer? Or knock first
like peddlers?)

Carpet ruffled, shoes kicked aside
computer, DVD player, video camera all gone,
fingerprints on the icebox in the basement
where six beers were consumed, brown bottles
rolling into the icy chalk-like dust
of the furnace room's open maw

. . . when it occurs to you, the diamond ring
your husband gave you ten years
too late — you never expected it
of him — you took it off

regrettably, your hands were dry, the lotion
grunge between the interfaces
of the stone's interlocking gold teeth
(placed in the velvet store jewellery box for safe
keeping) gone now ever after

two years later
fear before or behind
the locked door, standing
with the key in your hand

at the front door while
you're still out at the mall
wondering what may be happening
at this place you call
home

since that day you returned, opened
the door . . .

                    x!!

Fear in the narrow aisles
of the economy aeroplane after September 11th
(twin towers ablaze crumbling under flames
amidst the wagging of a billion tongues,
your neighbour on the telephone
and the child beside you
fast-talking in your ear

while one last unidentified Icarus falls
on a back page of history and memory
flailing arms and legs, falling
implanted horrific
mythic on your brain).

A tall, well-dressed Arab walks out
of the cubicle of washroom and
your own recalcitrant heart slurs over
a second, messy beat. That glazed eye
meeting the upturned faces on re-entering

silence grips the aisles on this flight
could be construed as something
of a fanatic, and the foreigner's needling look
across three seats from you bears you
an instant grudge while he reads

it in your blanched face and
you who have prided yourself
on your openness and light

are left to quick-chat with a neighbour
about crop blight
(about which you know
absolutely nothing) with staged
nonchalance.

        x!!!

That this apple is a globe
a world unto itself, perfect
as the one that rolled by the wayside, fooled
Atlanta (who thought she knew

what she was doing
like us all thought she had time
could make a run for it and

still win the race)
or that other Golden Delicious
that caused discord
when Paris gave it to Beauty
instead of Wisdom.

But as I bite into this Sobey
apple's unblemished form
the pale flesh is corky as old snow
flaccid, tasteless and, like Tantalus

who ate and drank without
fulfilment, this genetically-altered strain
enlarged and beautified, does not satisfy
but secretly returns what ill
has been done to it, releasing
chemicals from fertilizers and agents
out of the depths of Morpheus' realm.

I would grow another kind of apple, un-
adulterated inside my own back fence
except the fumes and poisons
from industry and warfare float
all the way from Paradise

between the borders of war
to enter this twisted nostril of nightmare.
Meanwhile the forests are burning in Africa
and South America and the nocturnal eyes of animals
fluorescent among the trees are disappearing
to be replaced by caged replicas and plastic toys.

We live in boxes

Me with my 2" square pad and list to do:
Fill the car with gas, buy groceries, replace
the broken light bulb in the fixture over the kitchen table.
You puzzle over the interest rates for *Sun Life* or Clarica
and the mortgage averaged over the next
four years to buy this split-level or that
two-storey (two boxes set alongside for largesse
or placed one atop the other as closer
to the sun) doing your own calculations
in minuscule letters on the lower half of the envelope
to a letter asking for donations for diabetes
or the blind, and one son

at the computer building skyscrapers
on Sim City while the other does his mathematics
complaining about the endless lists of the same
where mistakes accumulate in the boredom
of the white room with the square
picture window that cannot be opened

to let in the fresh of day
though the sky out there is blue
the air here laddered in dust motes that aim to travel
at an angle through the glass inside the window frame
to the awful presence of the sun or
moon spinning invisible light

stops short at the interstitial rays
where birds thud, break their delicate spines
against our incessant, invisible squares
and cunning surfaces that promise depth and the sunny future
when all the seasons remain secret inside the gravel trough
beside the spindle-legged September flowers
alongside the brick wall soon to be heaped over
with leaves or snow that turns to water in springtime
washing away all that has lived and died

and come to dust inside our tidy squares
waiting to be marked off
as the great events of the day on the grey sheets of newspaper
with the narrow columns for the Births and the Obituaries
or on the technicolour square that broadcasts
news of still far-off bombings

to all of sunny suburbia
while three blocks down to the graveyard
with the tidy plots of grass and the rectangular headstones
the ethereal light dives like a bird
streaming through, inexplicably, penetrating
the seamless surfaces even as the light

coming through our picture window
hypnotizes dust motes inside the dead white room
travelling towards the treacherous glass pane
magnetically drawing us up, up
through the fictitious frames of our boxed-in worlds
into a reflection of beyond.

The Secret Lives of Trees

i

A tree spreads outside my daughter's window
tells her not to get dressed don't bother
time stands still moves on the same
as the wind outside the glass, rain pit-patting
down, rustling silk inside the golden leaves
everything will happen as it must without
you or me but you really must get up!
You will be late for school! Your new brother
in the cradle on some wind-blown tree top
dreaming amid the chatter of birds
inside the lexicon of leaves
hardly an excuse (it seems).

ii

Along the driveway to the car,
a burgeoning of branches my husband must slash
(whose soft vegetation shades my wind-slurred thinking)
gets in his way, whips his face, makes him hack off
arms and legs thrashing in front
of his path needs to be chopped off!
And a twiggy tree between the cement squares
inside the fence slats beside the house
in the anger of time
and continuity may actually crack
the house's foundation

my neighbour agrees with him. I plea to keep
the red-berried rowan alive for the birds in the air
whose flight carries my eyes and thoughts across the sky
(the tree a shelter from the squareness of our lot
in its division from our practical neighbour)

while you vote for the house, ignore
ill-omens of the faerie mountain ash
with its spriggy message someday
to be found inside the city soot
and dust on Mount Ararat.

iii

The dogwood outside my front door
is a blessing each spring, its fragrance of soft, white petals
lingering in the dark entrance way with the rows of muddy boots
after I have shut the door on rain or cool sunshine
and bent over to flip off my soaking wet shoes.

In the summer the same small bush
lost in the foliage of the tree
next to it, nondescript
in a hedge beside the house
while the flower bed's loud pinks and
garish reds waft colour along

the brick wall; but when the light fails
and the season of darkness and greater
darkness encroaches — the tree a wiry scramble
twisted as Medusa's head full of snakes
between a flailing sea creature
and a twiggy-legged monster, lashes

some secret fear and turmoil
within the growing absence of light,
nurtures a panic only the body knows
what the brain denies in this modern age
of the right-angle and artificial heat
that something's out there

more than an ice age (winter
but a pause before thought). You remember
delivering the newspapers in the blizzard
last year? my fingers froze, you ahead of me
invisible in the white-out, with your backwards
shouted words *skip that house it's off*

the list lost in the icy mouth of the roaring
north wind so that I had to clench forward against
the slant of snow to face what lay ahead.

Night Leaving
(for those who have waited for lovers and loved ones)

In the wind, a leaf swirls by —

You told me you'd call
before dark the leaves piling high
against the back fence

after dark.
Why is that crow huddled there
in the squall?

I hear the leaves
(you'll laugh) that seem to sigh!

Bending to the car window
I kissed you goodbye. You said
you couldn't promise anything at all

the roads being slick, the leaves
piling high, and the rain turning to slush
and sleet.

Something must have come up
the pavement quicksilver, the roads sheer ice

In the wind, a leaf swirls by —

You said you'd call
but the telephone poles are dead trees blown down
and the internet's not working, goddamit!
I read the news in the morning (leaves — intricate
and filigreed, ash and elm — outside the door in a foreign code,
unreadable at my feet). I'll phone you said

when I can I'll call
before dark, but the leaves are piling ever higher
against the back fence after dark
growing light.

I know you couldn't call but, Why?

Sitting under the wind
with a heavy coat of snow piling higher and higher
over the house such a lonely place
to wait

where not a leaf swirls by —
I do not know what is going on above
or below me.

Pass, crow
(for Ted Hughes)

When he arrived on his sister's doorstep
the day of his funeral, she told him
"But John Stead . . . you're dead!"

Vague remains found on the railroad tracks
huddled duffle coat, soft fedora
blown some way off
to the four winds, unmistakable
musty and worn in the empty bowl
of the hat tinctured with the sweat
of his head exactly like her brother's
she said to authorities come asking.
"And so, John, you must really be a ghost
to have arrived out of the blue
sky with only a wisp of white sailing through
that great big sea!"

Wry at the thought
of the other named "John Doe,"
John took the provisions and extra clothes
his sister packed him for September nights' cold
settling in, wheeled his rusty bike back over the valley
to his digs: a tarpaulin spread out extended with garbage bags
tied at the corners to an old wheelbarrow
by a small, bent-over tree in the ravine
beneath the highway overpass.

Strange thing that there could be another
'John' seeing shapes in the root-overhang beside
the creek bed dreaming dinosaurs out the bones of the cliffs.
Bugger that! Bicycling down to the trickle of water
full of Styrofoam and wrappers and whatnot
the refuse of houses and properties and
boundaries the birds have all thankfully
learned to ignore.

Funny thing is, second time alive
the world is bluer, the day-by-dailyness
or drudgering
to be enjoyed, every one!

Corner of Fleet and Victoria

Rolling down the car window
turning the corner, swinging past
this busiest of intersections, Fleet
and Victoria

we caught wind of a cry, and another
another, syncopated

cry
in the hot wind of Indian summer
where a dozen young bull calves in the semi-trailer
looked out the grill to dust and pavement,
a sea of lowing amid the swirl

and screech of cars, huddled
mass of their bodies backed up in this terror
at what lurched   ahead

in the sizzling heat
while we sat behind a square of windshield
looking across the road at the nearest
fast-food and gas station
to a reasoned left.

You think only of now; you are
an animal, but the edge
of terror
on a wisp of breathless air
unmistakable, and
pain is
the moment

a wilderness of a universe
seen through eyes behind a forest of bars

escapes a holey world
on a bleaker note
that summons me now.

Roofing crew

Cathedral of trees arching
over the hot black-sparkle grain of roof shingle
Psst! Much of suburbia is filled with thugs of crows
and magpies insolent in their ways, tearing open garbage bags
over there a yogurt carton acrid-leaking onto a soggy
cereal box and banana peels scattered across this usually tidy
street on garbage day. Three weeks on strike
and mayhem inside the straight-edged
suburban block.

The slanting roof lines
all angles measured against
the plumb line of horizon, a point of faith
or for departure. The ramp inclines from the roof
to the truck overlapping the sidewalk, amber light
on the cab top signalling action with
a warning surreal beep beep,
the shingles all pre-packaged

in boxes trolleyed up the slant
of roof-space to be sectioned off
into squares filling up the larger square
of measured roof top and solid sky
beneath the backdrop of measureless blue
veils of drifting clouds.

The men, bare-backed, brown, young
or early middle aged, loud radio with the rude announcer
and rock music blaring in tune with the pulse of their blood
the tug of the absent moon and stars.

they feel, think little or something
about as they squat on the black roof, crack open
their bright aluminium lunch boxes at noon, toss crusts
to crowdom and magpiety
                          the oily blackcrows   who flutter down

                    take   anything they   can get, less than

        grateful

                              Cawr! cawr!

There was a Man . . .

with a moon-shaped bald-spot
waxing on top of his head who lived
in a rented room on the second floor
of a brown brick apartment block
in our neighbourhood built
near the school

three-and-a-half miles from the high office towers
where he worked inside walls before the square of a computer screen
(his shaved bald brother the one who sold cars at the corner of 9th and Dewdney)
leaving work for home in his pewter sports car at 5:04 pm
to watch the square of his computer screen, ham-and-cheese sandwich
in hand playing free sell or looking for southern lonely hearts
on MSN well past midnight
moonlight creeping through the cracks under
the sealed window panes, the L-shaped
room with two rectangular rooms
set at an angle, air conditioned

for summer; heated after October 1st when he'd go
to bed tossing and turning on the square
of his king-size water bed (his X
living inside a box in a nearby city) unable to sleep
for the music of the stars grinding below the brainstem
every time he'd slow to drowse
so what he'd have to drag

himself out of bed
to a silver stream under the tap
below the window in the kitchen
to stare at the full moon (the moon may be blamed
for such incidents) punched the pane
with his bare fist
(would need fifteen stitches across the knuckles)

Police sirens alerted, soon
on the scene . . .
While the girl in the almost windowless
room hermetically-sealed for changes
in temperature next door
was found the next day beaten up
by someone else she thought she knew.

Trespasses

Teach your dog to piss
on your own lawn. Wizard of Oz voice
behind the balcony (when you notice
the *Weedman* sign official on the lawn)
Young Sammy clutching the doggy bag, hopeless
in his hand as he dodges
from this side of the street
to the other side

around the corner
past the tic tac of houses of earthen colour conformity
brick and shingle, the new-tarred driveway
nicking the swerving black road
curving in some artist's landscape
of winding pavement stream

over-flowing October leaves filling the curbside
plastering drains by the sidewalk   yellow leaf light
illuminates the grey day

                jack rabbit, still
                as mottled stone

ears raised antennae shooting up straight
entering some wilderness of your own wandering
thoughts at the turn

in the road and the season
and the world
having crossed the grassy curvature
of ravine and the danger of highways
to trespass on our boxed-in suburbia, stopping
whiskers twitching, briefly
before hopping off . . .

By the rear wheel of the car
parked ahead where the sidewalk slants
for the driveway, this pink leather wallet, face down
new driving license, credit cards
and a handful of change   scattered . . .

When asked

to write a paper Kate asks for all the details
of the assignment
sure to have the parameters of the subject
marked and clear while Brad forgets about it
or doesn't want to know
invents his own.

14-year-old Robin Hood from the East End
(on a dare and one of three things initiates must do
to become one of the gang) stole
from the new liquor store
the size of a city parking lot. It's the planning
and cunning required by the prank, *he says*, that counts.
Liebfraumilch up his big sloppy sleeves or Mateus
inside his tatty hood draped from his wiry arm
because he *says* he can't stand those guys

don't need it like his dad
with the hairy, crooked toes sleeping in the armchair
clicking the remote, betimes
would smile and tap to rock's jagged beat
with a beer in hand and a fart
between construction jobs

on unemployment, and perhaps through a scavenger's instinct
in his blood-line inherited from a noble line of horse and cattle thieves
when trophies were the measure of the man
(or else through a persistent pedigree of petty robbers
and red-haired foxes trespassing on farmer's radiant blue
                                                    and yellow fields

slipping into the open maw
of the barn and the law

where maybe he wants,
taunts
human contact).

So this is it?
(*Mary's mother's words*)

"All he does is slap his hand
on the bedside table that wings out
in front of his sagging chest and sigh
and slap the table again," I complain about the an-across-the-hall's
habits to my daughter, Mary. The man who writes
lists of invisible numbers
on the cafeteria counter figuring out how to spend
a million dollar lottery ticket he can't get out to buy
so cheerful in his imagined good fortune
I tell him to spend it all while he can
and he winks at that one.

"What did you have for supper, Mum?
Did you have your supper yet?" Let's go over
to the lobby where the large woman on the next
sofa makes bread weaving it through her flabby fingers
gnarled as braided loaves on the table for all to admire.
*Would you like a piece? No thank you. Thank you
very much.* Looking through the sheet of glass
onto the open field listening to the ice crack
inside the balls of my joints through the seepage of blood in the creek
of my hip bones, I'm suddenly bright and far away
immersed in the dazzle of white, the smell of snow, its moist absence
and immense memories . . .

"Mother," a face beside me says, and I'm scrambling
in the white of thought for a grain of sand in the snow
to come up with the right name, "Mabel, did you come
to visit me at the Paradise Estates?" Fancy that!
when I realise my mistake and this is Mary

not my sister who died ten years ago.
Some days I'm carrying a mountain on my back
most days cannot look over my shoulder
on the way down the tortoise hump left

behind that wins the race on the way past
eighty-six. When the heat and your blood pressure are up
you *must* not get out of bed by yourself you *must* wear
what is laid out for you *do* not venture *too* far down the hall, *a bell rings*
wind shrilling through icicles hanging in winter branches
tinkling through the tangles of my thoughts snagged above my left ear
as I make an awkward scramble, clumsy walker and all
out the Emergency-Exit-Only door

I have been eyeing for weeks.
When my daughter comes back to visit me in bindings
next Sunday I start to feel sorry for her, but then
she thinks I'm drearily
not here some days, and that's why
I'm most stuck. There's a haze above my right eye
I can't quite make out for the wafer of the sun
through the smudge of cataract forming
like a bird in flight —

Sometimes *(for all those who have showed me*
the box, in which.............to sign my name)

                    the golden rays spiral down
on a cog of sunlight wheeling the hours and days
and months and years to lure me out from under the hunkered shadow
                              over the square that is my house
on the square of green or brown or white that is my lot
penetrated by a dark stub of driveway
paved straight in this *cul de sac* of life off
the grey block
                    of writing on this densely-written square of page
that speaks out the side of its straight-lined mouth
about logic and how to complete registration
to enter such and such a rite of passage or heaven/reward
when out of the top of my head

a string of words   out of nowhere, catches on a snag of wind
                                        hang-glides

against probability
climbing into the tall, tall prairie sky
zig zag to some zenith clairvoyant as hell's bells
under the furrow of my brow and the shadow of my hand
where some hawk or handsaw rides the wind
above the checkerboard of houses on square lots
above the black line of highway
over the fenced off farmers' fields

then the words jumble, their random-
ness runs, nets   the atmosphere, hurls   me off

                    . . . the last line of square cement sidewalk

in a whiplash of tangential (pre-)
cognition.

Among the poplar leaves, sometimes birds

flip green, flash gold   mirrors
leaves   transformed to fire
by sunsets crinkling
brown at the edges, dropping through
the diaphanous summer air

sifting through the simmering
between the flapping ears
sinking through the lustrous dirt (rich composted
in detritus of leaves where fronds extend forked tongues of bactilli
licking faces into the podsol), hidden flash
of DNA
stored in a twist of matter
activated by light and sun
and Water

inside this particle
seeping through the creep of toes
travelling up the wooden torso
reaching deep inside the veins of arms
feeding the fingered leaves of generations

(among which, birds
from time to time, dive   flash gold
connecting synapse to synapse
startling thought
alive
in leaves, like mirrors —)

You remark on something and
I remember thinking the same thing

seeing a pair of starlings dive
behind your eyes

blackpinkblueiridescent
and we are both delighted.

The summer that was a dream, when I woke up

Against the checkerboard of days and nights
we travelled the white-striped winding road
of July into the hot wind of August blowing in the car window
where the dog lolled her panting pink of tongue
to arrive at the beach, sun-blasted
in light, the tar-black parking lot
under the raw expanse of sky
in the jaw of the cove

across the raspy tongues of sedge grasses
over the burning sands scorching our feet
down to the lake ever-rippling, stippled blue in the distance
lapping brown tongues
coloured by the corrugated sands
in the mouth of the lake bed
The moment of ice cold
on the tip of your toe
that is warm, a moment later . . .

The summer my son grew a long arm
and a couple of hairy legs, a whole head taller
in the waves
      walked back to shore
even his little brother tousling in the waves
no longer a baby
      while his sister reading a book
           under a tree
woke up in a dream
with Tamlin, a boy wild strange and beautiful
in her arms calmed to gentleness.

The summer I fell asleep in the sun
and woke up to the dazzle of day
become blackness tossing heads of trees

torn apart   lightening rods, streaking white
bursting open   the freshness of snapdragon and marigold
in the cottage beds and the quiet rose

so fragrant beside the parched rock   drenched
ashen-smelling at the corner of the beach
where the sand meets the snake grass
and turf.

Nothing prepared me for Winter

The trees yielding their bare arms up to the sky
with a turning to something like prayer

twig mark footprints
by the side of the garage from a passing, small bird
looking for seed, and stories of snow

Nothing prepared me for winter
though the geese had been talking
all through October among the golden leaves

by the slate grey lake that mirrors the sky
where in a V of purpose everything

should have prepared me
for winter the trees themselves
had been talking about all summer long

late into October barely a breeze
though the air was brisk enough when sunny
some days

the deer mice tunnelling through
some crumbling orifice inside the thick, brick walls,
the chaos of cupboards and the musk of fear
their gnawing at night
inside my bones.

And driving over the highway overpass
that saws the curve of the land in two square parts
to my right a farmer's field where a fox cuts across

the trail, catches a scent of someone walking
slides off into the sedge grass where the ice
just thick enough to pass over

undetected to the other
side, and I in my old white car
have reached the turn off

never noticing the light that is always red, turning
green with a pause that turns to prayer
as I linger too long   a thought

about the stillness of trees
in the chill morning light the car behind
me, slamming across

black ice into the trunk of my car —
My skeleton trembling with something like a turning to prayer.

Nothing prepared me for the violence
of winter
            the wrenched bird neck of accident
of the unforeseen ahead

when you are a bird who cannot find seed
when you are a mouse in the dead of winter
inside the frozen ground

with a fifty percent chance of survival
when you are a fox who can or cannot
cross over the ice
                    to the other side the wrinkles
of worry, the cracks overwriting our lives

and the means of your death already written
in the skeins of the wind wrapping arms around you
at the turn of the road

although you had been told
and believed the world was always green
or golden

had only heard stories of snow
told by the wind that blows
sideways

drifts and piles high
inside yourself and the land.

Thought, unbidden

i

I would not like to dictate.
I would not like to deprive you; you have
your daily urges I have encountered

on the wings of the stair
and over the kitchen sink, you have come up
from behind, strong arms around my waist

so that I jump up
or stepping out of the tub, you appear
around the corner as I pull

a fresh towel from the hallway cupboard
(the children boisterous in the room below)
They'll be all right, you'd insist.

So, you see, finding myself sick and at odds
with myself and the world
I have just dreamed myself dead, and woken up
afraid.

I would not like to dictate.
I would not like to deprive you; you have
your daily urges I am well

aware; but what would I do peering over a dream cloud
streaked bloody or sunset-pink, fiery flames

to see you walking hand in hand with some other
over the curvature of earth?

What would I do?

ii

An acre of snow is an acre of snow —
some might argue differences
in slope and incline, but topographies of field and slough and sedge grasses
remain mere details: the visiting bird within the white frame
inside the field all that matters
(I like to think)

The particular heart beat
(within)
the shape of 'bird'
making all the difference.

So how can there be more than two birds
on a white background
without noise?

The heart and wing beat
of the departing bird, last breath
on the remaining's white face?

iii

What would the first bird meeting the third bird
in the white of heaven have to say to her? And
what would the second bird, flying
into the first bird, flying
into the third bird, say
to her? to her?

Geese mate for life, we've been told
and like to think, but love, like the wind, drives us on, perhaps
to change directions, north to south, or south to north or

with greater subtlety, northeasterly
to seek out some icy watering hole and driving interest
or southwesterly, simply to explore the tepid crave
of some new strain of reed in the feeding grounds.

Still the polarity of north-south and south-north
only apparent in the largest picture
always wins out, doesn't it?

Let me say, not more than a dream away
you are still the craggy boy with curls
thrumming on a guitar I found myself
sitting beside on a plush burgundy seat
in the golden glow of Louis' pub
waving a long-stemmed wine glass
in my white, almost unused hand
like a stunted wing.

Heart

I Think of the heart as a pump

says the nurse to the cardiac outpatient group
pink fist on the screen wired with red and blue arteries
like a battery, and this man beside you

whose presence made your heart skip
a beat in the midway university cafeteria
the tenor and rumble of bass in his voice a steady stream
pouring forth on urban planning and poverty and economic housing
for the poor

made you start up on an elbow
when you first picked up the phone
in your two-room basement apartment
the next week

held you pinioned
to the warm thud of his heart
beneath a red tartan shirt and
his young man's firmness during
the closest dance in the MUB

has two decades later
become a tightened fist of the will
angry and resigned, threatening the recalcitrant physical self
whose instant response, a squawk of indignation when,
say, in bumper-to-bumper traffic
a genetic time-bomb ready to spark, shorts
the circuit

on the way to work.
He is visited by the shadow of early morning
as an angel's tap on the left shoulder
and a burning twist as if to say, "You are mortal

and a liability to yourself. Turn around
and take note of the eight o'clock view
as for the first and last time

and of yourself, faded and greying: it is bleaker
and the sun most watery and uncertain, the heavy snow
saturating your heavy heart to a slow slide thump
and there is going to be negligible cheer this black
cough into
the backdrop of December . . .

II *You saw your heart bouncing*

 all over the screen like a lolling dog's tongue
on a happy day, or a Mexican jumping bean
swishing from side to side. All the work
a heart does in a life time!

Wet fish in the sea
held up by puppet strings
of built-in organic purpose
self-designed by natural selection, the strongest
most functional in-shaping the future of the species
amid individual infusions bestowed by some Fisher
who, let me remember, bestrews
as well as fishes
in the sea of things
and, of course, the invisible impulses
intonations
set off by ourselves, our bumpings into
or bouncings off

each other
amid the iridescences shining deep within
the dark water —
Life's stirring in chemical translation.

Remember the first heart's fist
and spark of life your daughter
on the ultrasound, pulsing light
across a dark screen, rising out
of the sea of non-being
                        into our futures?

III   I am having a heart attack

Chest weighed down, tectonic plates shifting
equilibrium shattered, tsunami of blood surging forth
racing in your head, ringing in your ears.
The vessels branching through the tree
of your being woodened with the plaque of living
surfeit in the veins, *I've had it*, you said, again
and again with problems at work, driving the kids to school
on time another problem not to mention bumper-to-bumper
traffic home exhaust trailing heavy in the frigid air
trapped among the idling
cars, nostrils burning and the ugly black snake ahead
surely an ill omen.

*IV   You never had a heart
attack . . .*

The angiogram clear, arteries
in the tree of yourself branching
unimpeded, irrefutable as the mule deer
antlers hung for a coat rack
as a reminder of our differences
behind the garage door —
your red tartan shirt thrown carelessly down
as everything else

lost
in the cloakroom of ourselves
(our comings in and goings out)
But you are the hunter who might have looked through the rifle
at the deer lifting her lovely head
wide-eyed and amazed.

The heart is a black hole in the electric trail of stars
orbiting the familiar planets among us.
The heart is not the problem.
Actually you never had a heart problem.
Just a pump, and a way around
the problem.

The heart is ever a new
star bursting into
song — a new
start. Can be.

Rose in March
(for Peter)

Daily I am learning I do not know all that I know.
The rose is beautiful though I do not know why.
With its soft symmetry, one marbled pink
and yellow lip of petal curling
towards where the sun once shone
down through maybe a chink of metal
link fence in a distant grower's garden, and I am learning all
that I know I do not know.

Why the rose leans this way and not the other way
and why I am partial to your warm presence, first toe
under the cool sheets to touch me
in the morning and I, inwardly blithe,
know I am not my own, or not only,
and I do not know all that I know.

When you return at the crease of day
with a hump on your back and woe
on your brow, all the muscles of your face written upon
for me to know your smile or frown by
and I don't know what to say
I learn again all that I see and know
I do not know or own.

And though we all agree the rose
is beautiful and someone else's sorrow
can be like our own, with the open air that surrounds and engulfs us
and a sometimes purposeful-seeming wind that enters our lungs
as we breathe in, may make us ask why
I can not know and do not know all that I know.

The rose is fragrant, fresh and pollinating in the wind just so
in your toe reaching across the cold desert of the bed I am touched by
the small animal of your pulse setting my heart aright
and I know that I do not know all that I know.

When one overcast March evening you surprised me
with a single rose, I breathed in
the truth and/or cliché to know the beauty of the world by
the earth smell and greenness that flowers red or pink
which I do not know at all that I know.
And all that I ever knew about the rose I have forgotten
or never did know.

Lilacs for Sandra

Lilacs outside the sliding glass
doors and spring, at last
wafting through the breezy screen
from the purple dreaming tree
when I notice a blight
darkening the nether steeples
stippled black-not-ants on high
the north side of the house, but
the tree luscious and purple
dressed in its finest, facing south
and it's spring. Spring!

That same lilac outside our window
ten years ago when we bought
the house I was thinking when
you phoned, and I told you how
I was just going to call you. My son
broke his finger when someone kicked his hand
when he picked up the soccer ball in the field.
Coincidence haphazard, purposeful jolts
in the nature of things: you calling me

when I was calling you. That's too bad,
you said, adding your own brief news,
an unexpected knot and gnarl in the life
of the tree that must redirect itself to carry on in the sunlight
and rhapsody of living, an unexpected double
beat to complicate the rhythm heard
only in the performer's ear. Well, that's too bad
he cannot play piano, but neither
could you, his piano teacher, for awhile,
you never said.

But the lilacs were still blooming
and it was spring and they went on dreaming
in shades of mauve and purple and darker purple
across fourteen octaves, treble to bass and bass to treble
the flowers on the table from the not-so-young spring tree
having been here for several seasons of memory
their fragrance wafting through
our own backdoor into the kitchen
of day-to-day living

and the tree quite strong, with elegant fronds
tapering fingers through the white fence slats
and over the triangular posts luring a symphony of birds and rabbits
from farther afield and farther and farther off, and I know

you will come through. Why?
because you are you, have long believed
in your students and overcoming obstacle.
By the way, the neighbour's raspberry canes
have found their way under the fence among
our rambling roses, their sweet nubs
promising fruit all the sweeter for having gone haywire
shooting through the matted, stone-netted turf
living through a world of winter and
knotted cancerous growth where
the rabbits chew through life itself
enjoying the bark as much as the berry
for a tasty nibble.

Meanwhile, please chase
the rabbits on a dream melody of lilac
to reach the notes of raspberry at the heart
of today
as I will try to do likewise.

Dragon poems

'I forgot to tell you . . . '

. . . must we "descend, ourselves to make
                           a couch — for whom?" *The Rubaiyat* xxii

I Dragons

are not beautiful. Although the iridescence
of a Dragon's scales, the metallic sheen
its righteous resolve, intricacy of its gear
at its nimble wingtips may amaze

A battalion of flaming yellow dragons across a purple sky
                           a hellish wonder to behold!

out of sight of its
        unseeing
gaze   the red blaze
of its fire may
mesmerize, I swear

a dragon does not see
                  with the flare
of its own fiery
        point of view

whiting out
during the Battle of Black and White.

II Dragons are awe-

ful. Their talons tear apart
human flesh   body parts
         scattered

to the four winds, across a desert
settling on a broken land their fiery breath
blackens fields, chars dwellings
leaves the wrack of lives on the cornices
of crumbling buildings, shrines   mosques

in the winter or anytime, water
a cesspool of contaminants
the old man and the child left
     in Basra to catch
         raindrops in a cup, falling

         through soot inside   the sky

step   on a land mine
just a toe-hold in the dirt   out of sight
crashes in darkness and flames.

Dragons leave   craters
in lives and livelihoods. But the benevolence of Dragons (gloriously
pre-announcing an intention to rebuild buildings   roads
the infrastructure for commerce with several odd billions
         after the war
they have been forced
to inflict) is well known.

III   Dragons

are vainglorious, traditionally empire-
builders, drawn to treasure hoards and oilfields
to refuel their fire and dominion over the Land and the Sky
will open fire at suspicion of a competitor
at armoured wing's length
                              remain
distrustful of Rats
who occupy oilfields (who may
go underground. Rats

                    suspected with/out
                              evidence

of suppressing information
and/or the truth: capable of using biological warfare
this Year of the Rat.

IV   . . . and a rat

having smelled another) wants
nothing more than to be
top of the Rat Pile.

A rat acquainted with Rat policies
may sit on the burning ship (contrary
to popular belief) so no one else
can have it (if he can't)

the other rats sneaking
in (surrounding
the oil hoard), not mentioning
a thing, really.

Dragon's wingspan and influence
fans multifarious, multitudinous interests and companies
45 (unnamed) countries bid for shares in the spoil to come —

V   *I forgot to tell you*

Dragons are rats
having acquired wings
having accumulated wealth and power
over earth and the skies
denominated heaven.

No one may boast
the fire and flare of wings
and power of a Dragon
without consequence.

(No, really. It takes
a Rat excuse to make
way for a Dragon.)

VI   *Dragons cannot retract*

battle along a narrow line of a border
280,000 troops waiting on the edge

of the desert sands, spreading
vast wings — without
losing (face)

radiance of fire from the missile's mouth
for dominion over territory and
her resources (who gets what?)

Dragons must declare war, plan
for the first missile to drop
at exactly eight o'clock
news time.

VII   Dragon Show: 8 pm

Between advertisements for weight-watchers TV dinners
          and Stayfree tampons, world viewers watch a country faraway

          as Storyland and *A Thousand and One Nights*, a camera
     tracks helicopters across the desert, glimpses sandstorms
tantalized by fireworks   cruise missile after missile flowering
magnificent
     over the mythical city of Baghdad as the moon under a sheath
          of cloud rising . . .

                              sails over the Tigris River.

Smart bombs
               by a narrow margin of lives, missing

          their target of opportunity,
          Operation Rat Freedom.

Underneath the TV frame of sky
                    the silhouettes of the living, barely
                         imagined, in the rubble below . . .

VIII   Elite Rat Guard

                send scud missiles across the desert
into the oil fields setting on fire a sea of flames licks the horizon
where the sun drops, red eye
pink sky

                                 watery
                    mirage   of an oil slick.

IX   When Dragons mind-

wash with blare radio: "Surrender
don't fight for a lost cause," a phalanx
of 8000 motley Rats carrying white flags

turn themselves in. Dragons
beguiled by the glamour of Might and Right
high on amphetamines and coffee and adrenalin
and fat talk of generals that keeps themselves up
while Rats with vestigial shoulder-blade wings, pinioned
pride strangulated, surrender

magnificent Dragon battalions
target phalanges of their rag-tag armies,
blazing their homes and their splendiferous city
with fat talk of generals that makes them swoop and whoop
and drop

high on amphetamines and coffee and adrenalin
Dragons beguiled by the glamour of Might and Right
and fat talk that keeps themselves up

when Rats flare hidden wings, turn
on Dragons   capture   confuse a few

of those pride-
                     ful
Dragons.

X   When three Rats

hold up white flags
draw Dragons
down black allies, push   them
into the swimming gutter
humiliated   prostrated   on the ground, gun
                             to the head.

(As in previous clip
Rat prisoners, this time
Dragon prisoners.)

XI   In retaliation, two Dragons

beat up two savage Rats
after a civil riot in another equally mythical city
one who spits in their surrender
                             faces, each swearing
                                  by his particular god
or absence (by body parts and
                their functions) beaten
                             with clubs
until the other's insolent body is
                             broken.

XII   When one Dragon

meets another Dragon   in mid air
black Tornado GR4   flying out of air channels, mistaken
for a flying rat enemy, tumbles
out of orbit   a choreography of writhing smoke fire!

        Oh glorious hell breaks loose!

(living beings   inside

                    the black entrails
                    of the   blasted
                    machine)

[Sometimes flawed: Tip One: Never think of your target
as other than a Rat. Never think of your target . . .
Never think of . . . Never think . . . Never.]

Outside the Aladdin Café

Awet drinking Turkish Kaffee
on the outdoor patio
puts his hand out
to feel the air

in a mythical city, visited by the grit of sandstorms
desert locusts and plagues, venom

of reptile spit, makes for a bitter rain
in a dry land.

No good leave the city, my friend
my brothers all kill lastime in the countryside.

East of Kuwait

in the swamplands, his cousin, Ahmed fishes
at Lake Hawr al Hammer   comes across
white-bellied fish, gelid eyes

                              gaze at the sky

soot-grey mosquito-spun clouds rise off the land
                    where there are   no insects

the Land after a decade of war

            like the hellish bottom of a river.

            Earth's insides, exploded —

Road to Baghdad

A pink wind blows over the desert
calligraphy of sand writing   escarpments
furrows of thought over
                    vast scrolled land
                         spaces

A peasant walking against the strength of wind
          clothes whipped
                    round, stick to
          one side of his body, his legs, his back   whirled
                    lines and folds, lift of
                         cloth, resigned
               determination —

The sand blows over the land
          along the winding road   *whiteout*
                    of houses

The sands blows over the land, filling in
                    cracks between
                         the tires

A convoy truck, bogged
down . . . A dry wind *higher than*
                    airports and heaven   *pinkish orange dust*
                              aura of god's will . . .

A black Apache helicopter hiccoughs. sand. between hub.
and blades of the propeller. clogs. Too dangerous
to continue someone decides. Six huddled, hunkered
down on the back of the pick-up truck
masked and grim. One soldier

holds his hand to his forehead, puts
a skittle in his mouth, memories
back home . . . The silk sand blows across
erases thought postpones
tomorrow.

Accident #13

An army tent laid close
to the ground, Bedouin style
out of sight . . .
the horizon pink with wind
of a *sharqi* spreading, red dust rising. . . . in spiralling clouds
mixing, indistinguishable from the fog of war
a coarse, grey blanket laid too close to skin and senses, burns
bare-naked nostrils, susceptible eyes water

the night   grainy
insidious pointillism of shapes and thoughts expanding
in phantom light . . .

Fear is an animal with a hundred watched eyes . . . A jeep coming over
the black, bumpy bank
of no man's dream —

(When no one knows where anybody is
in the bedlam of war with too many sergeants
following orders /or not
from above) just fallen
asleep when the tent is rocked
and someone is torn
awake.

   Hey what's going on!

     The moment before the vehicle runs through
 scrambling up . . .

    A roar of pain, unheard
through the thick of canvas and chrome and
of the other officers' fatigue

       . . . mowed down in the night.

Someone in the vehicle feeling the weight, the nudge
of something in the way, getting out
reluctantly.

Friendly and unfriendly fire

Accidents and incidents of friendly fire
are regrettable do not let them distort
your view of the true course of the war.
20 Blue Dragon soldiers
brought home in caskets

The nomenclature body bags for corpses
has been replaced by 'caskets' due
 to negative associations building up
with usage over time.
4 killed in action,
16 killed in friendly fire.

Sergeant K's words,"I had been trained
to protect myself from attack
from the front but not from
the side or the back. I watched
a Red Dragon in the adrenalin of the moment flatten a field of people,
two-year-old boy arms outspread in a V of alarm
                              sudden, momentary

                                        imploring

warning (how it was happening
to him) eyes, asterisks
the instant of fear before
                    he was hit

(his three scurrying sisters covering their ears
his mother in bundled skirts hunched over
the scrub grass   the chaotic cousins helter skelter
ingrained in my brain),"even twenty years
later.

On the parched lip

of the land
like a bowl, inclining

                tipsily

filled with dust
a scatter of lives wandering
children following behind, a baby

                   wailing-

outside the circle of an eye
glancing back and

forth
between plumes of smoke
acrid in your nostrils, oil fields set
afire by Rat Guard, deafening background explosions
display of the Might of Dragons incontestible.

Off to right of the road, someone
furtive, sharp sideways glance at yourself
or your comrade-in-arms, imagine
in the distance, neatly

             squared

within the binoculars' field, X' ed Rat snout
"Stop messing around," you order
on remote. "Stop him, Red #1,
stop him!"

"You forgot the warning shot."

Booby traps in the Persian Gulf

seeded under the waves the undulating ocean floor
like the roof of a Bengal tiger's mouth, land mines
(some left from the Gulf War
reactivated) planted
ready to explode off   Umm Qasr

sleek shadows flitting under the waves or arcing over
bobbing to the surface, sleek shiny heads
like a swimmer's seen from the distance
or a mermaid's to the susceptible
deprived eye

the dolphins and sea lions trained
to locate, un-bewares
army skin divers
devil may care

efficient
race-car driver men, skiers in avalanche country, test pilots
men who dismantle landmines, rescue men, firefighters, men who dare
when timing is critical, knowing
where and what
the risk

to do with nimble, fast fingers
quick / decision.

Aphrodite loves Mars

(Frontpage story in the Dragon Digest *more or less duplicated by the* Daily Dragon Meat-grinder News)*

A wingless female Dragon corporal
takes the wrong turn
through clouds of Dragon smoke and dust
into a Rat camp.

The bigger male Dragons backed
by a battery of artillery followed by cameras
with Head-of-Army Dragons watching her rescue
staged from distant armchairs
since princesses are far
and few

between
in war time (and gain
media attention, improve morale
among the troops).

Laptop Playmates on the WEB
virtually/not
the same.

Commander-in Chief Dragon's Warning to the Council of Rats
(and various eaves-dropped, conversations snipped)

I *Threatened Dragon rights, and clarified :*

"It is against Dragon's Rights Established by the Council of Creatures'
Convention to portray P.O.W. in humiliating positions."

"What about the Rats taken hostage? What about Osafa's Snakes?"

"Rats and Snakes don't qualify for Dragon Rights."

("But, but . . . the Dragon Invasion, itself, went against
was presented before
as a formality, not
to be taken
without the decision of the Council of Creatures!")

II *Lists of Ammunitions Found:*

2 Al Samoud Missiles banned by the Council of Creatures
found two kilometres south of the mythical city of Baghdad.

A cache of weapons of chemical warfare including gas masks
discovered outside the holy city of al-Najaf.

A case of banned chemicals on the ancient ruins of Babylon
undergoing tests —

"Those missiles, those masks are Dragon-made."

III *Further Conversations:*

"As yet there has been no sign of chemical warfare
or the ultimate, *Dragon Fire*."

"No sign? No sign did the announcer say?"

"Everyone knows Rats yearn for Dragon power to own
his own arsenal of Dragon Fire."

"But no one's found anything?"

"Waiting under our Dragon muzzles to be found, most probably."

The Mosque
(*Ali's words, attending prayers . . .*)

I pray to please, please have pity
what do we do to deserve, and there are gunshots

loud outside all around. The soldiers walk
in their muddy boots across the holy print
                                        prayer rug, defile
with their footsteps, on the dancing arabesques, the holy script
letters rising like dervishes — Those who drop

the bomb do not think   deafen
our sense, dull our kind thoughts

while the dead and injured pile up in the truck
outside. They walk this way, those soldiers

who walk, walk where they want
through anyone's prayer, Suryeesh and Hamin
and I stumble up
                        the anger rushes
in our blood — ten years sanctions we blame

on the west. The Imam raises his long arm, "Salem!"
Steps down three steps
                        in jerks
from the minibar altar that face the holy city
where the blessed prophet was born.

Our Imam, a thin man tall with the spirit
whose wise words cup our hearts in his outstretched

hands, he raises us up
and exhorts all Shea to cooperate

with the troops — leaders of men, they change
like the season   it is Allah's will
                                        whatever happen.

"Decisive"
(*Hind's words, reconstructed*)

Fear takes away, the body
not working. Already I bleed, it is just eight month.
Dark, dark silver the sky is lighted up
a mirror too bright reflects the sun
I don't want to watch.

Up and down the stair I go
up to heaven, no! Go back
to hell, better . . . I can't tell
the difference in darkness the noise
blasts my thought . . . Downstairs

safer, no upstairs! or I will be buried under! No!
downstairs! So I change my mind again, up
and down the stairs I climb, scared

my baby don't move no more.
I so scared I lie my face down on the cold floor, my mind sway
falling in darkness   chunk of building plaster flies by —
blood that looks black in the dark

Later the big noise   smoke pass over, and I go to the hospital,
"Please, please help me, I bleed," and they give me the C-section
but I find my friend there, she wait and wait and want
to have her baby too now. Now! Afraid, they tell her,
Sign here........this paper if something go wrong . . .

I name my baby Maarakat-al-Hawassen,
because they keep telling me the next battle
here in the mythical, majestic city
will be "decisive."

Dragon Report: Razing the Rat Airport:

I "The Coalitions Dragons will prevail . . .

"We dropped bombs over the darkened city, putting out the power
(a few buildings on back-up generators). In a surprise attack, we
surrounded the airport with tanks to secure reinforcements, were
driven back by gangs of thugs. We retreated several times to make
forays through the streets. We knocked on doors, a woman in rags,
gaping. The man at the next door spitting unknown blasphemies in
our faces. But we know we can go wherever we want, whenever we
want. And we will come back . . . !"

II Al-Jazzy Radio: Minister Mohammed Al-Rat warns
 "not to believe all the rumours . . . "

"As the undercover war drags on the Dragon Guard have paved the
road to Baghdad with skittles they say don't melt in the heat as if we
could be bribed and led by their tricks! The Dragon infidels forget
it is not by our stomachs we are led. Sad Damn may be dogshit. He
and his sons are dogshit, but he is our leader in the mythical city of
Baghdad. Last night he walked through the streets, slapped a fiver on
an outstretched hand, and held a curly-headed daughter.

The Dragon flyers that say WE DO NOT WANT YOUR OIL
fool no one."

Later . . .
Ab-grab prison repossessed by the Dragon Regime . . .

Posed and arranged to portray
the grotesqueries of war
a new wave *Guernica*, pile of bodies
wrenched into a parody of love
with love's toys

One culture's love goddess, Christina Aguilera
is Lilith in another, the pop tunes
that cloy.

Things happen in the dark, squirming
                    in the glare
the blinding blare of the camera light
            taboo is weakness

discovered, a wealth of rat-
dragon-ness twisted, blazing

lights exploit the dark
innards of fear, black-end
            splats of
                    disgust
over-exposed nightmares elongated
pumped phallic, wrenched
out of hand, dramatised
in technicolour with instamatic
instant gratification

for the exhibitionist and bored Dragon
underling demigod tired of the war
the incessant line of bullies with himself
near enough the top now
to give some of the orders.

Under prosecution six months later . . .
Corporal A blames Sergeant D
for giving her the orders.

Hate is

               an underground current that finds
    rivulets
  in the dispossessed. Hate is
a small burrowing street animal with fierce teeth

    the terrorist
  who digs two doors   one opening   here
    or somewhere else.

    Trapped
 between. Hate is
             the man forced to recant and
    the man forcing him. Hate is one faction, Shi'ite
    against Sunni, the details how to prepare meat or how to
wear a veil
  all important. Hate is two Imams — a traitor returned from exile
and the one who would represent the despot, deposed — just men
  in the lion's lair to be dismembered. Hate is

one people pitted against another, triumph
        of race over race. Hate is territorial, the boot
              on the face of the defeated hero.

              Hate is a child who has seen
    his parents blown up. Hate is

                 the next generation suppressed
            in our veins. Hate is

                     The rat inside
                    our blood.

Truth is . . .

I Front page

. . . the alacrity with which vandals
pull down the defeated tyrant's statue
Truth is the onlooker, reluctant
to partake, numbed
by carnage, elated madman
joy

that the bloodshed will end, at last.
Truth is the invaders' M88 tank finishing the job,

ramming in

the President's sculpture 'til it caves. Truth is
a river of blood, the wounded covering
hospital linoleum while electricity is run by
back up generators and water

is short
medicine and anaesthetics
looted. Truth is a foreign flag draped above
the statue until a quick-thinking soldier rushes up
to remove it (the media so easily

swayed), truth is
the accidental firing on local journalists
in the hotel (photograph of the decapitated
child an unnecessary weight
pressing on the soul
in the midst of jubilation, pictures of POW beaten
and humiliated

in definite bad taste). Truth is a gaggle
of soldiers walking through the President's palaces
with muddied footwear, someone's army boot smashing through
the President's portrait (records picture his foreign minister marching
across a poster of their own President a year ago). Truth is

a soldier slouching in the deposed's throne
what it would be like to live in such splendour
while the masses starve their own
White House nothing like.

II A Word with Tiresius

Truth is the most venerable of bystanders
an old man who has seen enough
dry-eyed
stands to one side of the road
to be interviewed by the too eager reporter,
his jaundiced view
this victory day

or Abdullah, the middle-aged mechanic
pushing his trolley to pick up bodies counting up
188 just now, doing this sad work for his god.
The desecration of the National Museum of Art
with its most ancient relics
of Babylon.

Do not speak of vainglorious Ozymandias
overlooking the desert (needing to be
taken down a notch) when once Gilgamesh
became more than a man
and, in legend, at least
grew wise.

Truth is a city of ruins

built on cities of ruins — the waves of invaders
searing the land with their own brief inscriptions
on time: Mesopotamia, City of Ur
Assyria, Chaldea, Babylonia,
Turkish, Mongolian, and Ottoman Empires
Persia and Al-Jumhuriyah and Iraq

most ancient of ruins, curious
crumbling structures by which to set a compass
or the clock by the diurnal eye
of the sun
in which to get lost   in the eye
sockets and broken jaw
of pillars
in the dry wind and heat
that sings

      but everything in the desert loses its edge

           yearns to be round on these dry lands . . .

The undercover war drags on . . .

I   Sometimes they shoot out

on a grey bystander, the movement
of a youth lying on his stomach
furtive in the dust of a dried up wadi
coming into town, having held off
for provisions, afraid

Sometimes they shoot out

at their own men standing in the streets
taking a wrong turn
at the intersection

                    so many countries, so many people
wearing alike the grimace of war
the smell of bitterness, many grappling particles
of dust and smoke linger in the air

the nose, the lungs
hang on your clothes, shadow
the buildings where you cannot see
sideways someone even now standing
beside you now behind
you about to kill

you in the side alley
maybe your wife and kid at home
across a world inside a distant dream having waited
through four-long months going on years
of fear

              an allied trooper
        out the corner of an eye spied

flying beside you in your patch of sky before
the brain registers . . .

II   . . . from the ambush

Someone (follower of the deposed
and/or God) raises a head
from the gutter, dynamite packed on his back
strides smoothly out
(or with what doubts?)

into the next world with what
others like himself (pride
to do the job right coming first
for who is afraid of life itself?) having
entered into a common cause of despair
organized among the youth
fervent with the present
that is the future at hand

or the middle-aged man
with a promise
for his family's safe keeping ever after
nothing much to loose

what were the odds he'd die
anyway in this outnumbered
war? As he drives the loaded taxi cab

through a wall without hope
blindly into the future
training himself to see through
the narrow focal point
of a kind of logic.

The Resources for Pain
(for Moazzam Begg)

Hogtied arms to legs shackled together
he was accused since found in the vicinity
escaped from the scene of action in Afghanistan
on the border of a neighbouring country
(his religion and sympathies marking him
indubitably) he did not know night from day

time passing in slow motion sped up nightmare
as the surreal mind in overdrive contends
with the artful influence of visible
and invisible

pain — kicks and bashes to the head and back
that do not exceed some power of healing
or camouflage before authorities
who look sharply

the other way don't want trouble
when not just generals (hard enough
to circumnavigate but those higher up)
urge the greater good remains
at stake — simple tests

of endurance reach to human limits like go
without food and sleep for five days in a row.
Noise and bright lights recorded rant insane about you
with the Interrogator in the white room ready at your elbow
with a prod and a needle filled with secret serum
orders you to drink twelve glasses of water in five minutes flat
to discover a sea of panic, nausea swell up

within you rocking obscenely lurid
on the greenish bile of no man's land.
(You are the guilty one!) And
must agree to everything
and be believed

for nothing
short of the worst
repeated in the precise words of the Interrogator
memorized in a sequence as for a strict teacher

and thus imprisoned for three more years
without proven charges you are moved
to a prison of the mind inside a faraway island
where you hear the splash of waves
as real enough will remember as a very hot place
within your brain's broiling under

a searing white spot of tropical sun
that wipes out overhead thought
under a searing white spot of tropical sun
that wipes out overhead thought
about who are you that wipes out
overhead thought three worlds ago
to arrive on the desolate shores
of this overexposed shadow
of existence.

The Mission has changed

With time to serve and a mission
before we return heroes to our wives and country
(remember the training-camp advertisement with
a photograph of an officer and his wife four-months pregnant?)
we came to the war-torn area with a view to hand back
the "jewel of the land" to those we'd been told
were the rightful heirs, and to zap

the enemy (having been brought up on video games
and such tests of skill.) But the black and white of the occasion
changed to subtler hues, a desert-sand austerity
the beige or puce of non-commitment, inadvertent
pain and grey, mostly grey with the hellish bowels
of the earth blackened and excavated in all the shanty towns
we dimly remember the reverent, sunken eyes
and swarthy face of another arch villain on the billboards
and television of our memories some thirty months ago
purported to have wanted to blow up
the western world, the countenance of the present
fades into the shadows of the past
so that the difference might prove

a trick of the mind. *So what* that we came
to uncover an arsenal and cache of weapons
designed to destroy the world, and failing
that, to blow up the spot of ground
on which we pictured the Mastermind standing
in his long, white robes inside a cave whose rigid passageways
withstood our occidental point of view and the crude targets
of our explosives as a way to out-manoeuver
our secret purposes. Now it all comes back.

We had been ordered to set our Targets of Opportunity
on the buildings of his office, disband his armies and
build two hospitals to house those injured
in this war of justice. But the Mission
has changed: we have been ordered to re-recruit
those same armies we disbanded and to rebuild
the hospital we blew up

while the horse-thief-cum-dictator shakes his white-clenched fist
in the courts of justice where the judge and jury glance up

and quickly down
to avoid the smouldering black eyes across the room
from where they are thinking, such a ridiculous sight!
and befuddled, too. I wonder is he sane
or our Mission changed again?

Notes

1. (p.8) *New and Collected Poems 1931-2001* (Harper Collins, 1988, rpt 2001), p 589. and *The Poetry of Pablo Neruda* ed by Ilan Stavans (Farrar, Straus and Giroux, 2003), p 221.

2. (p.10) "Distances": The "word" is supposed to have created the world in many mythologies, including God's word in the Bible. In Egyptian mythology, Ra's thoughts become the various gods in the Enead.

3 (p.13) "Risking the Avalanche": This poem was written after a group of teenagers were killed in an avalanche in February, 2003. Not to deny the tragedy, the poem is an attempt to understand the mentality that leads human beings to take such risks against better judgement. The teenagers had been warned that the area was unsafe but continued with their plans. Nevertheless, it could be argued that such risk-taking and extending limits has allowed humans to evolve as a species.

4. (p.20) "Phobos v!": Xerxes, the Persian conqueror, and Alexander the Great, the Macedonian conqueror, both faced the ill omen of an eclipse, the one carrying on with his campaign and the other delaying it.

5. (p.34) "Pass Crow": The title comes from Ted Hughes poem "Examination at Womb's Door" in his *Selected Poems: 1957-81* (London, Faber), p 115. The character John Stead is modelled on the real case history of the tramp, John Dane. Dane's funeral had been scheduled since what were mistaken as his remains were found on the railway tracks.

6. (p.63) "Dragon Poems": Any perceived resemblance to the US-led Invasion of Iraq must be a reflection of the reader's own thoughts.

7. (p.72) "The Road to Baghdad": Two types of wind are famous in the desert: a *sharqi* is a dry wind from the south — usually occurring at the change of seasons — can gust up to 50 mph (80 kmph); *a shamal* prevailing from the north and northeast between June and September heats up the land and cools the air.

8. (p.78) "Commander-in-chief Dragon's Warning": Osafa is either the evil uncle of Aladdin of the Magic Lamp or his alter ego.

9. (p.80) "Decisive": This story is a reconstruction inspired by a news story about a woman in an article in the *National Post*, entitled "Coalition bombing disrupts new deliveries in hospitals." Her baby was named Maarakat-al-Hawassen, translated as "victory is decisive." A6, April, 2003.

10 .(p.82) The painting, *Guernica*, by Pablo Picasso dramatises the carnage of the Spanish civil war.

11. (p. 84) "Truth is Frontpage": A photograph of the American foreign minister stomping on the portrait of Saddam Hussein is pictured in Angela L. Mance's. *Iraq* (Philadelphia: Chelsea House Publishers, 2002), p.82.

12. (p.90) In "Mustapha and his friends", Paul Bowles describes as the "most monstrous absurdity" for the Moslem "to fear death, the future. or the consequences of one's acts, since that would be tantamount to fearing life itself." *Their Heads are Green and their Hands are Blue* (Harper Collins, 1984), 61. I have tried to go beyond this stereotype.

13. (p.89) The poem "The Resources for pain" is provoked by the capture and torture of Moazzam Begg who escaped Afghanistan and was located on the border of Pakistan perhaps on the way to Iraq.

GILLIAN HARDING-RUSSELL has two collections of poetry, *Candles in my Head* (Ekstasis Editions, 2001), and *Vertigo* (River Books, 2004). She won first prize in the poetry section of Saskatchewan Writers' Guild's short literary contest in 2006 for "Roses, Lovers and God" judged by Tim Bowling, and, in 2005, first prize for "Nothing Prepared Me for Winter" judged by Susan Musgrave. In 2004, she also won second prize in *The New Quarterly Review*'s "summer theme" contest for "Among the poplar, sometimes birds". Her poetry has been published in numerous literary journals across Canada and she is a frequent reviewer for *Event* and *Prairie Fire*.